CLOSER TO A YES

A Founder's Guide to Getting Noticed by Investors

By Dar'shun Kendrick, JD/MBA

Book Dedication

This book is dedicated to my WHYs—my parents Daisy and Rick Kendrick. They showed me the POWER in serving others and the POTENTIAL for creating generational wealth through entrepreneurship.

This book is also dedicated to each and every founder, raising capital or not, for your bravery in stepping into the unknown. You all inspire me every day.

Table of Contents

Preface. Why I Wrote This Book…..*Page 4*

Chapter 1. The Founders' Kid…..*Page 8*

Chapter 2. An Overview of Capital Raising in General…..*Page 19*

Chapter 3. Why It's Important BUT SO HARD to Get to a Yes from Investors…..*Page 41*

Chapter 4. How To Get Closer to a Yes ASAP: Your Guide…..*Page 48*

Chapter 5. So What Now…?…..*Page 60*

Chapter 6. My Sincerest Wishes for You and Beyond…..*Page 72*

Conclusion. Resources & Follow Up…..*Page 75*

Appendix. Guide…..*Page 76*

PREFACE: Why I Wrote This Book

Well...

Where do I start?

First of all, this isn't my first book—or second, third, or sixth.

This is my seventh book! I wrote several books in high school that are still unpublished. They are sitting somewhere around my home office collecting dust, but I keep them for nostalgia. I am an introvert, so I love putting my thoughts and dreams on paper. In high school, I was REALLY an introvert, as I was really unpopular and had few friends. These books were my refuge from a world I couldn't escape—at least until I went home.

I have published one book: *Morning to Motivation.* I wrote it during the COVID-19 pandemic to inspire a hurting world based on the positive influences in my life. Some influences came natural like my mom who taught me I could do ANYTHING (and I believed her). Some influences I developed, like making five positive affirmations each morning. This book still available for pickup at your major booksellers and, no surprise, Amazon. I am convinced that half of successful entrepreneurship is inspiration, which I talk about later in this book. The other half of successful entrepreneurship is perspiration, which this book is about in detail.

So why am I writing THIS book at THIS time and actually PUBLISHING it?

It's simple: I am tired of repeating myself. That's right. I am a Type-A person, and repeating myself is one of my least favorite activities. I know I have to do it to remain an amicable person. But, secretly, sometimes I wish I could take out a tape recorder and hit "play" at the right spot anytime someone asks me the same question I am asked all the time. Even better, I wish I could pull something from the sky and give it to them in writing. Oh, a girl with a Type-A personality could only wish her life were that efficient. But I have a solution.

THIS book!

I figured with almost two decades of experience as a corporate attorney, years as an investment advisor representative, years arbitrating for FINRA (Financial Industry Regulatory Authority) and helping companies nationwide raise billions in private investment funds, now was the time to write down all the advice I have given verbally, in writing, by smoke signal, loudly and subconsciously after all these years. I figured if my advice is in writing, I will not only be satisfying my mythical dream of providing "on demand" physical documentation but doing some good in the world for so many founders.

On a more personal note, my *why* extends beyond my personality. You see, I have a personal and professional mission of helping at least 100 people become millionaires by 2032 through entrepreneurship. In order to do that, I have to help companies experience significant growth. To experience significant growth, most companies need to raise capital from investors. To raise capital from investors, companies need to lead investors to saying "yes" to an investment in their company. To get closer to a "yes" from an investor, companies have to be "Investor Ready" when the investment opportunity presents. To get a company to be Investor Ready, certain steps have to be taken first. You see where I am going with this?

I have a disclaimer, though (of course I do): I have never solely raised capital for a business I have fully owned. I have raised funds for a commercial real estate syndicate that I started with four other black women in 2020. I have helped thousands of companies all over the United States raise billions in private investment capital. I have sat on so many panels and given so many presentations on capital raising that I cannot keep up. However, I value transparency, particularly when it comes to founders and this capital-raising process. I don't want you to think I am some sort of serial, multitalented entrepreneur out here raising billions for my own businesses. I am not. This fact, however, doesn't make me any less qualified to speak about what I talk about in this book. This is just noted in full transparency to say: You can do it, too, without being a serial, multitalented entrepreneur. Or maybe that is you. If so, congrats. If not, join my club!

But what I can tell you is that I have helped thousands of companies directly and even more indirectly with their capital raises through legal compliance and business coaching. I can also tell you I see the SAME issues and gaps in knowledge reoccurring when it comes to companies being ready to raise investor capital. This is because I spent 13 years only practicing securities law, this specific area of law. What I was able to compile over the years of experience with clients, investors, and everyone in between is absolutely the best comprehensive advice I could ever give.

Now, I wish that I could promise everyone reading this book that, after you are done, investors will be knocking down your door. They won't. Why? Because capital raising, as I often tell founders, is a mix of art and science. I can give you the science—the facts, "best practices" and data—but only you as a founder can carry out the required art of capital raising. You are the one who has to forge relationships with potential investors; you are the one who has to show leadership to your team; and you are the one who has to do the hard parts consistently every day. I can only help you with half of the equation. We do have business coaching classes to help you put together and formulate the art portion of capital raising—but, at the end of the day, we cannot force you to take action.

So, this book is for those of YOU who want the science behind capital raising. It's for hungry founders who want to raise capital from investors but are looking to bypass all the mistakes that I have seen clients make over the last 17 years as of the time of this book being published. The goal is that, if you can bypass and plan around the mistakes that I have seen others make, you can focus on growing your company. And THAT is the one important way of getting closer to a "yes" from investors.

Chapter 1. The Founders' Kid

A Tale of 2 Founders: My Why

August 28, 1982. A star was born. Or at least I'd like to think so. I was born at Grady Memorial Hospital in Atlanta, Georgia. Natives just call it "Grady" and, yes, I am a "Grady baby."

My parents were super young when they had me. My mom was 20 and my dad was 21. I cannot even imagine having a child at their age, but those were different times then. In the '80s, the focus was on getting a nice job and having a nice family. I don't remember much from being such a small child, but others living during those times tell me that entrepreneurship was still considered a bit weird and certainly unstable. Venturing off on an adventure to start your own business was seen as something "they" did—not average working Americans. Which is why the fact that my dad was an entrepreneur during that time is all the more fascinating.

My dad's stepdad taught him the ceramic tile business around the age of 16. As of the publishing of this book, my dad is still going some 40+ years later. He is a master craftsman in the ceramic tile and marble business. If you follow me on social media, you will see that I post his work every now and again. The level of detail and care he gives to his masterpieces are inspiring to say the least. He has worked on some of the most famous buildings in Atlanta, from high rises to apartment buildings to luxury homes. When I saw my dad work, I saw someone moving in their calling with the type of mastery and care he gave to each minute of his work. He is like a surgeon performing open-heart surgery when he gets a piece of tile in his hand, a wet saw on his side, and a design in mind. Imagine! He has been working with his hands crafting works of art in the homes of people for longer than I have been alive. If it takes 10,000 hours to become an expert, and my dad, who is the hardest-working man I know, averages 60 hours a week, then my dad has been an expert for about 44 years. Longer than I have breathed on this Earth. WOW!

My mom worked retail jobs when we were small and always had a passion for kids. It's three of us. I am the oldest and only girl (and cutest). I have two younger brothers. Because she loved kids so much, she always wanted to do work around them if it was paid or unpaid. I think her love of kids is one of the reasons why she doesn't understand why I am in my 40s without a kid in sight. Sorry, Mom. But she expressed to me how she loves their inquisitive and innocent minds. When I was starting high school, she opened up an in-home daycare in the bottom of our home. Unfortunately, the facilities were right beside my bedroom—that didn't help my ovaries want children. I helped my mom after school and the summers. What I remember the most is that there were a LOT of rules. I guess I could see why: You are dealing with the most vulnerable human population. But seriously, I could write an additional book about the regulations and expense of running an in-home daycare. From my mom doing the accounting, I remember this point the most: The margins were super-low. Even as a teenager in high school, not having taken one class toward my MBA, I knew that the margins were low and unsustainable.

Why am I telling you all this? To let you know that my entire childhood was composed of serving my parents, both entrepreneurs. It became a step of whom I am to support and serve people that believed in the American dream and wanted to be their own boss and drive their own destiny. People just like you reading this book! My parents are the reason that I am not only the person I am, but that I am passionate about businesses. I saw them go through the ups and downs of entrepreneurship, including legal issues that needed resolving, but they could never seem to find the right lawyer who understood and cared about their issues. They certainly never brought an attorney around me that I felt had the expertise in business to resolve the issue or who looked like me—a natural-haired black woman with a determination to help the culture by any means necessary. So I did what I've always innately done when there is a problem: I committed to solving the problem.

I made a decision in the fourth grade to become an attorney. I knew that I was good at analyzing situations and making compelling arguments. I also thrived in reading and writing, winning competitions and keeping my own journal at a young age. It didn't hurt that my cousin had told me lawyers make LOADS of money right out of law school. That was empathically NOT true, but I digress. In 2000, I enrolled at Oglethorpe University with a focus on political science (my second love) and communications. Not specifically a pre-law track, but I figured what could be closer to the law than policy and communications?

When I enrolled at the University of GA School of Law in 2004, I thought, "What specific type of lawyer did I want to be?" In law school, there are not necessarily specific legal tracks like there is in undergrad. But I knew the value in becoming a specialist, so I wanted to be hyperfocused on the outside activities and classes that I took. All this would lead me toward the type of attorney I wanted to be.

Because I had been involved in politics since I was 18 and seen injustice after injustice after injustice … this can go on for a while … I initially wanted to be a civil rights attorney. But I soon discovered that particular area of law (1) that didn't pay back these increasing student loans fast enough for me, and (2) most lawyers don't start out as civil rights attorneys or practice that exclusively. They essentially evolve into these roles by their main practice of civil litigation or criminal law or as a lobbyist. The path wasn't as straightforward or as lucrative as I had hoped. So, back to the drawing board.

The math wasn't going to add up enough for me to become a civil rights attorney, so I decided I would be a lobbyist. I had worked for two members of Congress and worked at the Georgia State Capitol for a committee chairman for two years. I ran a state senate campaign and worked on various campaigns throughout my pre-law school years. Surely that was the best path forward. Well, I soon discovered how tight-knit that circle of governmental affairs professionals was, and my hopes and dreams were dashed when I couldn't make any inroads. Any inroads that paid anyway. See reason No. 1 above about how that wasn't going to work for my bank account.

But God was about to step in! It was my 2nd year (2L as we call it), and I needed to fill my schedule with the appropriate credits toward graduation. So, I read a description about a class called "Securities Litigation and Enforcement." I read the description in the course schedule, and it sounded interesting. I had never heard of securities law and didn't even know what a security was, to tell you the truth. I guess I never thought about how companies get money to grow their business. We didn't discuss money or investing or financial planning at my kitchen table growing up. I think I just assumed that businesses either self-financed, so they didn't need money, or people just gave businesses money without any strings attached. Or maybe the business sought a loan. I am not sure what I thought, but I had never heard of securities law.

Long story short, I took the class and fell in love with securities law. Like over the top, where have you been all my life, I think I want to marry you type of love! It was like my eyes were opened, and something CLICKED inside of me that said "This is your calling." So, I took every securities and corporate law class

I could while in law school. There were not many classes, however, as law school tends to train you to be a litigator. But, that didn't stop me from reading the Securities Act of 1933 and 1934 on my own. I was even able to take an accounting class at the UGA Business School that counted toward my law degree. And when I did that, I discovered a dirty secret for someone to be in law school: I actually liked the BUSINESS of law more than I did the actual PRACTICE of law. I decided to get my MBA, but I was ready to leave Athens, Georgia. I ended up getting my MBA from Kennesaw State four years after graduating from UGA Law.

In 2010, I started Kairos Capital Legal Advisors after a few name changes. "Kairos" is Greek for "at the right time" or "at the appointed time." This is how I feel about life and business. As humans, we can only do so much on this Earth and in real time. The rest is up to God or the universe or whatever spiritual beliefs you have. So, when companies are raising capital, and it gets frustrating, or when I am getting frustrated with my own company, I remember *Kairos*—everything happens at the appointed time.

Does my childhood story sound familiar, Founders? Was there was a catalyst that prompted you to become the person that you are or do what you do that you can trace back to your upbringing? Or maybe you were in corporate America, and you either got frustrated with the culture or saw a problem that needed solving, and you fell in love with being a problem-solver. Every founder has a story. And I always tell founders that your story is your strength. It's your strength for when you want to give up, like we all do from time to time. It's your strength for when you have to make decisions that are counter to your belief and value system. It's your strength for telling the outside world what makes you so special. Embrace your story. Tell your story. Live your story.

This is MY why. What is yours? Let me tell you some valuable and powerful lessons I learned from my parents as business owners.

The Lessons I Learned: My Top 9

1. **Get a GREAT team.** A company is only going to be as strong as its weakest team member. A GREAT company is made up of GREAT people. A MEDIOCRE company is made up of MEDIOCRE people. A BAD company is made up of … you get the picture. So hire slowly and fire quickly. It's the best thing you could ever do.
2. **Focus on REVENUE.** Cash is king (or queen). Full stop. We don't barter by corn or cows; we barter by cash. And the way to get cash is to get sales, which bring in revenue. "Every day, in every way, make money." The bells and whistles of a company are toppings. Revenue is the ice cream. You don't have a dessert without the ice cream. Focus on the bottom line and ask yourself: "How can I make money today and long term?" Rinse and repeat.
3. **Learn something new every day.** Never. Stop. Learning. This is something I totally owe to my mom. She not only made sure I was studious and tried my best in school, outside of a formal classroom, she challenged me to learn more every day. Learning doesn't have to be a whole skillset or anything formal. It can be a podcast or a book or anything. Just add a new wrinkle to your brain. Once you stop learning, you stop growing and you die along with your company.
4. **Lead Wisely.** You are the person who is ultimately responsible for the decisions that you, your company, and your team make. Lead by example. Even when you think team members don't notice, they do. Even when you don't feel like it, do it. Even when you are tempted to do

otherwise, don't. As a founder, you are like a general marching his troops out to battle. Where you walk, your troops will follow. The decisions you make can be a matter of life or death. So lead and lead wisely.

5. **Rest as needed.** Honestly, this is my constant battle. How much rest you need depends on each person and each circumstance. Find out what works for YOU and be intentional about when you rest and the act of resting. We were not meant to work 80+ hour weeks, no matter what the pundits and social media says. You cannot be your best unless you rest. So do it. Schedule it. Stop everything else.

6. **Ask for help.** This is another battle of mine. We are not an island. We cannot reach and scale great heights on our own. Seek out strategic partners and work beneficially in those relationships. Take an honest assessment of where your gaps are in a company as far as talent and skillset. There's a person who has a solution for every problem you are facing. You just have to be willing to ask for help.

7. **Focus on customer service.** It sounds like an old piece advice. But, although the customer may not be always right, you need enough customers to produce—what? Revenue. Focus on making as many of them as you can happy and watch them turn into an ambassador your company. There is no growth like happy "word of mouth" growth. So, make that an objective of every step of the customer process of your company. Watch your return on investment grow.

8. **Give back**. If it's one thing my parents were consistent with is giving. My parents are some of the most-giving people who ever lived. Yep, I said it. I stand by it. You are in business because you have a particular gift to share with the world. Don't be stingy with it. You have to focus on revenue, but where there is space and an opportunity to give back to your community in some way, do it. It will

come back to you in miraculous ways. I am a living testimony.

9. **Believe in something BIGGER than yourself.** Whatever your religion or non-religion, believe in something stronger and more powerful than yourself. For me, that's God. As you may have already learned from this book and about me is that I don't do anything apart from God. This isn't a Christian book, but Christ will make appearances. My mom is the daughter of a preacher; my dad's mom is the praying grandmother we all need and talk about. Just because this is the last lesson, I don't want you to think this is least lesson. I just want to end these lessons on a great note.

I am certain there are about 20 other lessons I could write down in this session, but for time's sake, these are my Top 9, the guiding principles, which can become the building blocks of any successful company. Keep these in the top of your mind. Write them down and have them readily assessable for everyone who is a step of your team. If you are faithful to these principles, they will be faithful to you.

Why Am I Am Who I Am

For those who follow me on social media, you know that I am up at 4:00 a.m. every morning. Weekends, holidays, and vacations? I MAY sleep in until 5:00 a.m. if I've had a late night. But, for the most part, every morning my body pops up at 4:00 a.m. As you would expect, this annoys anyone who has the tragedy of sharing a room with me. So, it probably comes as no surprise that I am asked: "Why do you get up so early?" My honest and consistent response is "Because I love what I do!"

I believe that each day is filled with NEW opportunities. But we only see these opportunities if we look hard enough and be alert to their presence. Every day is as unpredictable as the next. No matter how much I plan my schedule in 15-minute increments (I really do), life just happens without my permission. Because life is so unpredictable, it's exciting to me. So I just wake up excited about each new day. Yes, there will be the normal roller coaster rides of entrepreneurship we all go through. But isn't it the view from the top of a roller coaster hill looking down into the unknown that makes life worth living? There could be a mud pool at the end or a pot of gold—you never know! No two days in anyone's life are the same. I truly believe that our lives can change SUDDENLY and MIRACULOUSLY at any moment. Therefore, I approach each day with this hope and expectation. I hope that, as a founder, you learn to do the same.

My adult experiences have influenced who I have become just as much as my childhood upbringing. Practicing law for almost 20 years, I believe I have seen it all….. *almost*. In these 20 years, I have consistently seen injustice after injustice in terms of access to private capital markets and in receiving private capital. These injustices aren't just limited to those who look like my community, but far and wide to anyone who is not a white heterosexual male. Yes—I said it! The truth hurts, and it is what it is. But there is NO WAY I am going to have this unique skillset and let those injustices continue in front of me. In the words of my mom who quotes the Bible "To whom much is given, much is required." I am required to use what I have to do what I can do.

But to do this, every day, I must make a decision to get better. How do I get better? My continuing to learn more and more about my area of legal practice. My continuous learning takes various forms, depending on the various times I can fit in a lesson. I like to vary complexity in the subject matter by learning a variety of subjects. I am determined to be the best I can be so that I can pass this expertise and knowledge to those who need it most. No mediocre white man can say I don't belong. They still will, but at least they won't be correct. I've heard it said, and it's very true, "Somebody in need is waiting on my obedience." What do you have to offer that someone desperately needs? You know what it is or you wouldn't be reading this book. So be obedient, Founder! Build that company. Someone—group, community, nation, or world—is waiting.

For example, in December of 2023, I completed the Blck VC Institute Cohort. I am actually still surprised I got it. It's a highly competitive program that is free of charge in order to get more black venture capitalists, executives, and others into the ecosystem. We can complain about the startling facts around venture capital funding for people of color and women. But the way to alleviate that is to have someone on the other side of the investor table who looks like these underserved and often discounted founders.

WHO I am? I am God's obedient child. Put on this Earth to answer someone's need by my obedience. That's why, in the summer of 2024, my firm launched Project Esther, which is an initiative to give one year of free legal advice to up to three black-led venture capital firms. Someone had a need. Those firms don't have to wait on my obedience any longer.

I say all this to say that, as a founder, you have something so special that you are bringing to the world. Something that is so unique only you can do it. That small voice and passion that prompted you to start your company or, like me, wakes you up super early every day is there for a reason. It's your WHY and your WHO of what is going to carry you over the finish line to growing your company and raising capital from investors. Listen to that voice and nurture that fire you have burning so brightly within you.

Now, I don't want to be disingenuous. I have a fair warning: CAPITAL RAISING IS A JOURNEY. One that is frustrating and tiresome and annoying and exhilarating and rewarding—all at the same time. However, making sure you know WHY you are and WHO you are will sustain you as you ride this roller coaster journey. If that means you need to write reminders on sticky notes and cards, do it. If you have ever been to my home, you know I have sticky notes and quotes and pictures everywhere. Because we all need visual reminders when things seem to not be going our way. Those little moments of inspiration keep us going for another day.

For those of you that are Christian believers like me, I will reiterate that it's important for you to remember WHOSE you are as well. You belong to the Creator of the Universe, to an omnipresence (all present), omnipotent (all powerful), and omniscient (all knowing) person who is with you throughout life and beyond. So, call on your Father for the help you need because you understand WHOSE you are in this founder's journey. And when you call on Him for help, he answers.

Chapter 2. An Overview of Capital Raising in General

An Overview of the Regulatory Scheme

How about that S.E.C.?! No, not the Southeastern Conference for all you sports fanatics. I am talking about the Securities & Exchange Commission. I want to take some time to give an overview of the regulatory scheme so you understand comprehensively why it's so hard to raise capital from investors at times because of the laws and rules you need to comply with to be legally complaint. I also want to equip you with a general understanding and history of capital raising in the United States.

Ever since 1934, the S.E.C. has been tasked with protecting the investing public from well-meaning AND fraudulent issuers of securities when they are raising capital from investors. The S.E.C. was authorized by the Securities and Exchange Act of 1934 after the 1929 Great Depression saw a lot of financial disasters, misrepresentations, and mistrusts happen during that financial period. The Foundational Act for the initial issuance of securities is the Securities Act of 1933, but it's the act a year later in which Congress authorized the S.E.C. to promulgate rules and regulations around capital markets.

The S.E.C. is the federal regulatory authority whose main job is to regulate public and private capital markets and protect the investing public.[1] The balance the S.E.C. has to strike is to encourage investing in founders to spur the U.S. economy and,

---

[1] https://www.sec.gov/about/mission (last accessed 7/23/24)

at the same time, to protect investors. I don't envy their job because that's a thin balance. I noted that the S.E.C. protects investors from BOTH fraudulent issuers of securities or companies but also well-meaning ones. That's important to note because I think a lot of people think that, as long as they are not doing anything fraudulent or intentionally misleading people, the S.E.C. plays no role in their capital raising journey. They do. I assure you, they do. It's very possible for a well-meaning, nonfraudulent issuer to do something that is within the jurisdiction of the S.E.C. to regulate AND that the issuer does something that violates an S.E.C. rule. In other words, you can be a well-meaning founder, and the S.E.C. still believes there are protections you must provide to your investors, even absent fraud or fraudulent intent. I want to emphasize this point because I have a lot of prospective clients who think that, just because they are doing a private transaction with their church group, somehow the S.E.C. isn't authorized or doesn't care about their investment transactions. They do. Many times, I simply advise audiences to assume that the S.E.C. has jurisdiction over your transaction or securities unless you can find a legitimate reason why they do not.

As you can probably see, I could write a whole book about S.E.C. jurisdiction, citing case law and recent decisions pulling back the jurisdiction of federal agencies, weakening their power to make rules and regulations, but we don't have time for that in this book. Instead, let's just say that the S.E.C., in general, has jurisdiction over transactions that are raising capital from investors unless you have experienced legal counsel that can advise you otherwise. This is a simplistic way to put it because something has to qualify as a "security" for the S.E.C. to have jurisdiction, then there are exceptions to this rule, then exceptions to certain rules even though they have jurisdiction and you have to qualify as an actual "investment." Sigh ... I just mentioned this so you know it's a lot more complicated and nuanced than how I have stated it, but I don't want to turn this into a law school book. Let's move on.

Whenever I am speaking to groups of eager founders—those eager to jump right in to soliciting investors for dollars—I have to be the party pooper (I mean, that's why people pay me actually: to be the risk-adverse, negative voice in the room). I ask the crowd to leave with this principle if they don't hear anything else I say. Remember "2+2+2". This stands for 2 choices, 2 layers, and 2 things to do. I implore you all to remember the same.

2 Choices
Whenever you are raising capital from investors, there are 2 choices for raising capital legally (emphasis on legally): (1) Register with the S.E.C., which is a whole, expensive, and time-consuming thing; OR (2) Find an exemption to registering with the S.E.C. Those are your ONLY two choices! You'd be surprised how many clients try to find a 3rd choice or exemption to these 2 choices. They don't exist. You only have 2. Then, once you evaluated if you must register with the S.E.C. or if you are exempted, you must identify what S.E.C. exemption rule you will raise under. Once you have made that choice, the issuing company must make sure its activities going forward fall in line with the rules of that exemption.

2 Levels
Whenever you are raising capital, there are 2 levels: (1) federal AND/OR (2) state. Just because you file something with the S.E.C. doesn't mean you do not have to file in accordance with state "blue sky" laws, depending on your raise and where you are targeting investors—or vice versa: if you are filing something with a particular state doesn't mean you don't also have to file something federally with the S.E.C. or any other federal agency. There are certain scenarios in which a company will be exempted

from filing something with the S.E.C. and only have to file with the state or vice versa. But, as a founder, you at least need to understand that you have 2 levels of consideration for filings to consider.

2 Things To Do
Whenever you are raising capital, there are 2 things you must do as a company: (1) File AND (2) draft. You will need to file SOMETHING (what that is depends) with a federal or state agency or sometimes both, as I discussed above. You will also need an experienced securities attorney to draft your internal documents to protect you as a founder and your company. These documents are not required to be filed, but it would not be wise not to have them. And some internal documents must be provided to certain investors, depending on your capital raising exemption and your targeted investors. Failure to do either one of these can be catastrophic to heights you cannot even imagine. From the S.E.C. shutting down your ability to raise capital now, and, sometime in the future, to you waking up one day and realizing you no longer own a majority of your company.

Was that clear enough? Did 2+2+2 help you to at least get a sense of the basics you should remember when raising capital? Still a little muddy? Don't worry. You don't need to understand all the details—that's why you hire an experienced securities attorney to guide you through all this legal stuff. But the company is better, and you are better when you are an informed founder, so I hope it made enough sense. Moving right along.

Types of Capital

There are 2 types of capital generally (notice a theme here?): Debt and equity (ownership in a company). They are treated differently under the law, so it's important to understand their differences as a founder BEFORE you make any financial decisions. Just to be clear [*Dar'shun taps microphone*]: both debt and equity raises are under the jurisdiction of the S.E.C. for capital raising rules and regulations. It's a common misconception that, if you are raising debt by, let's say, a convertible note, you can do whatever you want with whomever you want in any way you want without going through the 2+2+2 analysis above. Remember, Founders, let's just ASSUME you are regulated whenever you think about raising capital and keep that assumption until you get a legal opinion from an experienced securities attorney, okay?

As with most choices in life, there are pros and cons to choosing to raise capital through debt. Debt is defined as "something that is owed or due."[2] Now, I know what you are thinking. Isn't an investor who invests in my company and takes equity also due a return on their investment? I know it's complicated, but the answer is not really. When investors invest through equity, they are taking a risk; maybe you will return their investment with additional returns and maybe you won't. Maybe you will go bankrupt. Maybe you will return less than their equity investment. Maybe…maybe. The law assumes that debt holders have a legal standing of being owed vs. equity holders who are not owed. Listen, I just work here, folks. While there is no crystal ball to guarantee that a company will return debt investments, if a company were to liquidate or dissolve, debt investors get paid FIRST before equity holders, including the founders and the largest equity investors. There are even levels of disbursement priorities within the debt investor pool. So, for the investors, being a debt holder has some assurances.

Another added perk for debt holders is interest payments. Think about your student loans or mortgage. Every month you pay something toward the principal and interest. The same is true

---

[2] https://www.investopedia.com/terms/d/debt.asp (last accessed 7/23/24).

for debt holders. They are holding a note, just like that student loan or mortgage. And so these debt holders are entitled to incremental payments on that total principal and interest as a debt holder. The frequency and terms around those payments are detailed in the legal agreements (that's why it's important to have experienced legal counsel), but this is an attractive draw as well to debt investors.

So why would a founder take on debt investors? Well, you get to keep more ownership in your company because debt holders are not getting any equity (ownership) in your company. If and when you do an equity round, you WILL be giving up some portion of ownership in your company. That's the rule. If an investor has none of the advantages of being a debt investor like I discussed above, they need something in exchange for their capital—and it is ownership in your company. And their hope is that you grow as a company, make a big exit through an IPO (initial public offering) or acquisition, and can pay them back in several multiples what they invested. That's the hope and the dream.

Dealing with equity investors is my specialty, although we deal with all securities. Why? Because there are a lot more nuances and details and math—*oh, the math*—that come from doing equity investment deals. I love it—even the math! Did I mention how much math is involved? Okay. So, as I stated above, if you are raising capital and giving away equity in exchange for an investment, you are giving away some portion of your company. The amounts are handled in the due diligence process and negotiations, but some portion of your company will be given away to investors, if you want a deal.

I have seen where founders will haggle over .5% or 1%—and I understand. As a founder, you want to preserve every percentage of your business you can for future capital raising rounds or for yourself and your future generations and maybe even future employees. But here's something to think about (which I always tell founders): 30% of a watermelon is ALWAYS going to be larger than 90% or 100% of a grape. Remember why you are capital raising in the first place: To scale and grow your business. Trust that you will do that, and the percentages will matter less in the future. Find that magic amount of equity you are willing to give up and, if it makes sense, seal the deal. Having an investor ready to do a deal is worth much more than other investors "you think you can get" by giving less equity.

Think about this rationally. Equity investors don't get first in line if you go belly-up; they get paid after ALL debts have been paid, not just to debt holders. Additionally, equity investors very rarely get paid dividends or consistent payments like debt holders. Listen—I am on YOUR side, Founders. This may sound like a session of this book dedicated to advocating for investors, but it is not. I see so many founders lose out on good or even great deals because they aren't considering the value of the investment beyond dollars or handling over things that won't matter a year from now. Don't let that be you. There is a method to negotiating and all sorts of creative ways to get deals done. Consult your experienced securities attorney to learn more.

In addition, you will see some founders who will do a capital stack that is mixed with some debt holders and some equity holders for a fundraising round. My head is hurting just thinking about the paperwork and math, but I am sure there is some accountant somewhere salivating over the math involved. I will leave it to you and your executive team, which hopefully includes an accountant and experienced securities attorney, to help you navigate deciding your capital stack. My job with this session is to give you a broad look at what could be as you build a great foundation for raising capital.

Stages of Capital

I mentioned before that I work with both founders of issuing companies and funders (who are also founders but general partners of venture capital or private equity firms). The stages that I discuss here will be different for founders and funders.

When founders start on a new journey of raising new capital from investors, it's called a "round." So, for example, if a founder has raised funds, stops for a period of time, and then decides to raise a new amount, technically they are in a new round of financing.

In this industry, we assign new round names: Pre-seed, Seed, Series A, Series B, Series (I have seen up to Series F). The assumption is that if the company has raised all those rounds, presumably you are a successful company. The next step is that the company either does an IPO (initial public offering) or gets acquired.

Depending on who you ask, you will get a different definition of what each one of these rounds mean and when you should raise them. For the sake of simplicity, I will give you my simplest view of rounds in terms of where the company is in terms of the development and growth cycle. For example, if ABC Corp. is pre-revenue and building out a prototype or MVP (most viable product) and looking for less than $50,000 from family and friends, I think most experts would say this looks like a seed round. Why? Because they are pre-revenue and building out a product and because of the amount they are seeking to raise. However, an established company that has revenue and is raising capital for the first time from institutional and accredited individuals would appropriately be categorized as raising a Series A.

Sometimes it's helpful to think of these stages in sequence of how many times there has been a raise, but other times, it doesn't make sense. Either way, what you call it is something you can determine with your team and others later. Let's not spend much time on that. Eventually, you will need to determine what type of round you are in because you will need to sound competent in conversations with investors, and also so you can focus your efforts on the right investors. Some investors, no matter how great you are as a founder or how much of a hockey stick for the trajectory of your business, will NEVER invest in a pre-seed round because of how risky it is. Other investors love investing in seed and Series A but nothing before or after. So it's important to know. You will get there.

If you are a founder of a company that is not a venture capital or private equity firm, that previous paragraph was for you. Now, let's turn our attention on funders, those general partners of private equity and venture capital firms. Whereas founders' capital raising is seen in terms of rounds, funders raise "funds" and the name of the round is more basic. There is no magic or analysis to be done to the name of these funds. ABC LLP will raise ABC Fund I then ABC Fund 2 then ABC Fund 3 and so on. Boring, perhaps, but simple to understand. At some point, typically these private equity and venture capital firms stop counting and you just see in the news "ABC Corp. raises another fund." Again, I don't make the rules, folks; I just work here. This book is focused on traditional funders and not founders as much, so that's all I will say about that subject. Contact me to learn more.

Infrastructure and Setup

Before moving into the regulatory exemptions, of course it's important to have your company set up in a way that is sound from a legal and business standpoint. Some questions to ask:

Where will you incorporate? Many venture capital firms set up under Delaware law because the corporate setup and tax code is very favorable toward investors or LPs (limited partners.) Many founders set up in Delaware for the same reason. Just note that wherever you incorporate, you will need a registered agent living in other states in which you are doing business for official communications to our business; you are also responsible for keeping up with any changing laws and regulations in that state.

What entity do you want to form? Hopefully, no one reading this is thinking about or operating as a sole proprietorship. In the age of registering your company online with such ease, there is no excuse for leaving yourself up to so much personal liability. However, venture capital firms and private equity firms are structured as LPs, limited partnerships with the general partners as the managers, and the limited partners as the investors. Most founders either form as a limited liability company (LLC) or C Corporation. There are some tax benefits to filing with the IRS to be a S Corporation, but consult with your CPA or accountant. (Sorry, I don't give tax advice.) If you are thinking about raising capital, most of the companies that are doing exempted capital raising on the S.E.C.'s website portal are corporations. Something to think about. The structure is easier and more established for investors than other separate legal entity forms.

What else? I experience many founders who incorporate and think that's the end. Oh, don't we wish but no. In most states, after you have finished incorporating, now you need a business license in the local jurisdiction in which you are running your business. Be warned! The business license process is lacking in uniformity or ease to understand or easily explainable. Each state, each county, and each city has different forms, deadlines, requirements, fees, etc. All you need to know at this point is simply incorporating is not the end.

Regulatory Exemptions to Raise

REMEMBER 2+2+2? Let's explore that a little more. You will remember that there are 2 choices, 2 levels, and 2 things to do when raising capital from investors. Let's focus on the last 2: levels and things to do, particularly filing something with someone. I will assume that you are not reading this book because you want to file full registration with the S.E.C. but instead want to raise funds privately through an exemption.

Below, you will see brief overview of the regulatory capital raising exemptions that are currently available as of the date of publication of this book. Remember, with some exemptions, just filing with the S.E.C. is sufficient. Some require filing with the federal and state. But ALL of these meet the first of the last "2+2+2 model" I laid out above: FILING. SOMETHING.

Accredited vs. Nonaccredited Investor
In this nation and under the S.E.C. capital raising regulatory scheme, investors are divided into 2 buckets. (Listen, I don't know why everything in capital markets seems to end up in 2s.) You are either an accredited investor or a nonaccredited investor. I repeat—there are ONLY 2 choices.

An accredited investor has a regulatory definition from the S.E.C. and includes individuals and entities. For the sake of this book, let's focus on the individual definition. It means that you have a net worth of over $1 million, not including your primary residence, or an annual income of $200,000 or more or $300,000 or more if you a couple, and it's expected that you will have that amount in the future and can provide evidence. You are also an individual accredited investor if you have a FINRA license of a Series 7, Series 63, and Series 65 (like I do).

So, assuming an individual doesn't meet ANY of the requirements above—then, they are a nonaccredited investor. Remember, there is no hybrid or in between. You are either accredited or you are not. So, as you can imagine, most individuals fall under being nonaccredited.

Why is this distinction so important? Because accredited investors are given wide latitude and freedom by the S.E.C. to invest pretty much in whatever they want, when they want, and how much they want. They aren't required to be provided with certain documentation because the assumption is that these investors or either savvy enough or have enough money to lose that they don't need the full protections of the S.E.C. Those that are NOT accredited investors, i.e., nonaccredited investors, have limitations on what they can invest in, when and how much and they have to be given certain documentation. This is one of the main reasons you see companies using regulatory exemptions that don't target nonaccredited investors—too much time and money can be spent on meeting the requirements when dealing with nonaccredited investors. As you can hopefully see, the distinction between accredited and nonaccredited investors is vitally important if you are looking to raise capital from investors. Your entire marketing plan will be affected by the regulatory exemption you choose and whom you are targeting—accredited versus nonaccredited investors.

I will note that there are two other categories of investors mentioned in S.E.C. regulation: sophisticated investors (which focuses on how long someone has been invested in the markets) and qualified investors (which focuses more on assets you have under your management or how you are structured as an entity). But, for the sake of this book, let's focus on accredited investors vs. nonaccredited. Want to learn more? You know what to do. Hit up that experienced securities attorney.

Reg A+
This exemption I call the "last step" before a full-blown IPO (initial public offering). This is why it's commonly referred to as a mini-IPO. It allows eligible companies to raise up to $20 million under a Tier 1 offering and up to $75 million under a Tier 2 offering. It's a similar process to doing an IPO but not as extensive or expensive as a registered offering through an IPO. There are reports to file on a continuous basis for Tier 2 and an exit report for Tier 1.

There are filings you have to do with the S.E.C. then wait on them to "qualify" you and requirements for your offering circular, which is the forward-facing offering document you give investors who qualify access to read about your company and offering. Then, if you are doing a Tier 1, there is an added layer of filings with the state in which you are offering these securities. Remember those state "blue sky" laws we discussed earlier?

Reg D: 506(b), 506(c), and 504
These are the exemptions that were used before the JOBS (Jump Start Our Businesses Act) was passed in 2011, which made access to capital easier. They are called Regulation D offerings because they are under session D of the S.E.C. capital raising rules.

A 506(b) private placement offering allows companies to raise unlimited capital from investors from with whom the company has a preexisting relationship and is an accredited investor. Issuing companies cannot use generational solicitation in this type of offering. What is general solicitation? It includes, but is not limited to, posting on social media, sending an email blast that's not targeted or screaming your offering into a random crowd. Anything that is not targeted and said publicly can be construed as a general solicitation. Companies can raise capital from up to 35 sophisticated investors within a 90-day period.

A 506© offering is the most popular in real estate and in general. This offering does allow general solicitation and raise of an unlimited amount. But ALL the investors have to be accredited investors, and the issuing companies has the burden of taking "reasonable steps" to ensure that the investor is an accredited investor.

A 504 offering is the least-used of the Reg. D offerings. It allows companies to raise up to $10 million in a 12-month period from investors whom the company has a relationship with. This exemption also allows what we call "testing of the waters," which is essentially a solicitation from a company to investors to see if there is interest from the market in investing into a company without triggering S.E.C. required filings during the testing period.

Reg. CF
Regulation crowdfunding (or Reg CF) was the hallmark of the JOBS Act, which was passed in 2011. The initial intentions behind Reg CF were to make it easier for smaller companies to raise capital without going through the S.E.C.'s intense compliance standards, i.e., getting more companies raising capital from investors and growing and creating jobs, expanding access to investments from every day people, and helping the overall U.S. economy.

Reg. CF allows qualified companies to raise up to $5M from the crowd—family, friends, and the public—within a 12-month period from investors online via the FINRA (Financial Industry Regulatory Authority) registered funding portal. Some things to note: You have to be a qualified company, so no investment companies or hedge funds. This is really meant for the small and less-sophisticated company trying to raise capital.

You can only raise $5M within a 12-month period; otherwise, you run into integration issues (which is an issue with ALL capital raises, but that's why you have an experienced securities attorney to help with this). You must also go through a FINRA registered online funding portal. So, you can't send potential investors to your website or an email address or even to a person on your team. All investors must go through a FINRA registered funding portal, and that funding portal has requirements in terms of investor education and back-office responsibilities to the investor.

There are some financial reporting requirements based on how much a company wants to raise (which can be frustrating at times based on the average Reg CF raise and its original intentions) and some ongoing reporting requirements to the S.E.C. However, overall Reg CF is meant to get companies raising capital from investors and deploying that capital to grow American businesses efficiently and as swiftly as they can. There are still some issues that can be addressed to make it easier, but it's certainly become more popular in the last years. It's also a viable option to companies that think they want to raise capital from investors.

IGE (The Invest Georgia Exemption)
I live, work, and play in Georgia. It's where my law firm/investment advisory firm is registered and where my family has been for generations. I say all that because Georgia has a very special place in my heart.

I would like to put this special note out there for Georgia registered businesses, even if you are a foreign entity registered in Georgia. There is what I call "Georgia's best kept secret" for companies who are registered in Georgia. It's an intrastate offering, which is an exemption to S.E.C. jurisdiction that allows states to develop their own capital-raising rules, SO LONG AS the offerings as kept in the state—intrastate.

The Invest Georgia Exemption (or IGE)[3] is something I have Georgia registered companies consider. There are some limitations, e.g., ALL investors have to be residents of Georgia, and *residents* itself has a legal definition. All money has to be deposited into a bank registered here in Georgia, which is not that hard if you are banking at any large bank or credit union. There is an 80% test where 80% of revenue, assets, OR proceeds have to be in Georgia. It's an OR test not an AND test so that's not usually hard to meet. But the form to do the compliance for IGE is literally three pages you fill out on the Georgia Secretary of State's office and email it. You can't get much simpler than that. Georgia is one of several states that offer this intrastate exemption for raising capital.

Now I always have to remind people with ALL of these exemptions but especially IGE: Remember 2+2+2. Just because you have taken care of the compliance portion of raising capital, you STILL need internal documents to protect you as a company, even though you have taken care of the compliance portion of the "2+2+2" model. No federal, state, or local agency is going to help you with that part. You need an experienced securities attorney for that. I know someone.

Documents Attached to Capital Raising

Okay. Now that we have gone through all the regulatory compliance, let's focus on Step 2 of the "2+2+2" equation of 2 things you need to do when raising capital from investors: Draft something. And that drafting is more somethings than just one document. It can go up to several, depending on the deal and

---

[3] https://sos.ga.gov/page/invest-georgia-exemption (last accessed on 7/23/24).

your company and any other ancillary things besides a capital raise that you are trying to do. But I am going to focus on only a few for time's sake. This could be a whole MBA or law school course honestly. But you can also visit my website or my LinkedIn profile to find insights on many of these.

The Offering Document
The offering document is what I call the "Bible" of capital raising. For those of you from another religion or none at all, pick the most sacred book you can think of in the place of my analogy and that is what the offering document is. The offering document is known by many names, but it has the same function. It's called a "private placement memorandum" (PPM), "offering circular," a "prospectus," or a "business plan." But, if done correctly, they all have the same objective: To protect the company from misunderstandings from investors and at the same time provide investors with a comprehensive snapshot of the company and its financial health and future plans. There are all sorts of disclaimers and disclosures in this document as well as information about the company and team. There are many attachments that can be financial reports and projections and addendums and graphs that explain information contained in the main body of the offering document.

The offering document can range from 50 to several hundred to thousands of pages. Everything you want or need to know about a company should be contained in this document. That's why it's so important—because if an investor gets amnesia about something, you should be able to point back to this offering document. And, at the same time, it provides the investor a good roadmap of how they will get their money back if they invest in your company. Hopefully, you understand now why, as a Christian, I call it the "Bible" of capital raising. This document is of upmost importance for founders and should be drafted with the upmost care.

SAFEs vs. Convertible Notes

If you are raising a pre-seed or seed round, chances are you are pre-revenue or have very little revenue. If that's the case, it's hard to put a valuation on your company. So many founders look to these two documents to help them raise capital in the very early days of their company.

A SAFE (Simple Agreement for Future Equity) is where an investor invests money in a company not knowing that company's value. When the company has an equity round (as I explain below), that investment converts to equity, which is why it's called an "agreement for future equity." There are a few kinds of SAFE documents that can discount the amount the investor has to pay for future equity and valuation caps for those first investors to retain as much ownership in the company as possible. But because these SAFE documents tend to be so simple to use, they are favored by a lot of startup founders. However, please note that, just because these agreements are simple, don't expect every investor to want to invest in your company using a SAFE. They are risky to investors in that founders have to actually have a priced equity round for the conversion to equity to take place. Some companies just do a series of SAFEs and delay or never have a priced equity round. There are some protections around this like a post money safe, but again, we are giving a general overview in this book. An investor who invests using a safe is making an investment of money and is investing without any equity or any return. That's different than convertible notes, which we discuss below.

Convertible notes, like SAFEs, are investments that convert to equity in a company at a later date. The difference is that convertible notes have an end date to convert ("maturity date"). Additionally, companies usually make regular increments of payment on the note during the term of the convertible note.

Think of your car note or mortgage payments each month. So, the investor knows that, on a certain date, they either get their money back or the investment converts to a certain amount of equity, depending on the terms in the convertible note. Because of these added bonuses for investors, the legal document is not as simple as a SAFE to draft. As with everything in life, there are trade-offs.

Equity (for priced rounds)
Now we come to the step that hopefully makes the above paragraph make sense: priced rounds and straight equity. In these rounds, once an investor invests money, they are automatically given equity (ownership) in a company. These are called "straight equity" or "priced rounds," as the investor is not delayed in receiving equity for a future date like with SAFEs and convertible notes. Most outside investors receive preferred stock, and even that has levels within it; most founders receive common stock, getting paid LAST in a liquidation or acquisition event.

These investors are vested and added to the company's cap table (i.e., capitalization table in an offering document) automatically as vested equity versus as an option or pending option. Additionally, to have a straight equity round, the company has to have a valuation, so these are for companies that know the value of their company. That means many companies that used priced rounds are post-revenue (otherwise, it's much harder to know the value of your unique company and offering). There are two (surprise!) different types of stock: preferred and common.

These rounds are therefore "priced" in that there is simple math used to determine what the price per share is. If a company is valued at $1 million, and they are selling 100 shares for 10% of their company, it means they are raising $100,000 ($1M/10%) and $100,000/100 shares is $1,000 per share. Now the math can get a lot more complex than that when you add in ESOPs (Employee Stock Option Plans) and options and unvested options, but let's just stick with this for now. (Did I mention how much math is involved in my practice of law?) And this all assumes the company is issuing preferred stock, like for the SAFEs and convertible notes, not the common stock founders usually receive. As you can probably guess by the name, preferred stock gives preferences to these stockholders by way of distribution and other rights.

Investor Rights Agreement

This Investor Rights Agreement, called by many other names, is meant to solidify the relationship between the issuing company and the investor. Hence, this is why it's called the "Investor RIGHTS Agreement." Typically, these agreements detail any voting rights and how those are exercised as well as liquidating preferences and rights and perhaps participation rights side letters allowing investors to participate in future rounds. I have seen it all in terms of what is put into these actual agreements and the side letters attached to them. So, while the offering document is the Holy Grail of capital raising, the Investor Rights Agreement is a close second in terms of importance. Whenever there is a dispute as to a company's actions or an investor's actions, lawyers will run to the offering document as a basis for what was communicated and then to this Investor Rights Agreement to see how it works with the offering document and what was communicated. This seems like the perfect time to underscore again how important it is to get an experienced securities attorney to guide you through how these documents I am discussing work together and apart.

Honorable Mention Documents

I told you before how you can have a few to several documents as a company during your raise. Here are some others, besides the ones above that I have generally draft and advise on as well:

- *NDA (Non-Disclosure Agreements).* I am sure you know what these are, but sometimes founders will require these to partner or from investors to discuss company information. They are tricky in that sometimes investors will flat out refuse to sign them. Very early on, as a team of a company, you will need to decide if that's a deal-breaker for your company.
- *Founders' Agreement.* The Founders' Agreement, as it sounds, is just an agreement between the founders on the relationship just among founders in terms of voting rights and day-to-day responsibilities and how to communicate or exit the company. That would be something to disclose to founders as an attachment to the offering document. Investors would need to know the terms of this agreement.
- *Non-Solicitation Agreement & Clause.* Non-solicitation agreements are sometimes stand-alone documents that founders sign amongst each other to prevent other founders from picking off employees or clients. However, most of the time if there is a Founders' Agreement, it will include a non-solicitation clause.
- *Noncompete Agreement & Clause.* There may also be a non-compete clause in the Founders' Agreement but usually you will also see non-competes with top, early employees. This puts temporary and limited restriction on employees and founders who leave and what they can do that competes with your company. You as a company and founder don't want to develop a product or secrets in your service business for someone to take that information, quit, and then set up shop as your competitor up the street. However, non-competes are becoming more limited in recent years, as the government does not like to restrict enterprise and someone's ability to make a living. Since non-competes are going to be based on state law, consult an attorney within your state for details.

- *Side letters.* These are exactly what they sound like—side letters that are not a step of the offering document or Investor Rights Agreements. However, they do provide certain side rights like the ability to participate in an offering if a founder or general partner does or to have the most favorable terms of a future round of financing, etc. They are just as important as the main documents, so make sure you and your experienced securities attorney take note.

Chapter 3. Why It's Important—but so HARD—to Get a "Yes" from an Investor

Company 1B

It's easier to go through the remainder of the book telling a story with a character. Let's name this character "Company 1B." It is a generative artificial intelligence company that makes it easier to produce financial reports and answer questions about the reports. Company 1B has a team of five founders, all with various backgrounds and expertise in not only artificial intelligence but GAAP procedures and management and leadership. So let's use Company 1B to answer the question posed in this chapter.

Company 1B has been trying to raise funds to finalize its product and hire more engineers. It has been having numerous conversations with investors from the east coast to west coast. Some leads sound promising, and Company 1B thinks it is close to a term sheet with one big investor. But why haven't they cut the check yet? Don't they know rent and payroll is due?

Why is it so hard to get a "yes" from an investor? If I knew the comprehensive, spot on, always correct answer to that question, I would be rich. Not just a little rich either. Elon Musk, sending people to Jupiter just because I have the money type of rich. The truth is—I don't know, so I am not even going to try and guess. I would rather lead you through a series of questions and comments. Then you can arrive at your own answer and adjust accordingly.

The reason I don't know why it's so hard to get an investor to a "yes" is because every investor is different, every company is different, every situation is different, and every market is different and...you get what I am saying. I know lawyers say "it depends" a lot as a stop gap for almost every question. But, in this case, this really is the most appropriate answer. I hate to say the old lawyer adage, but whenever a prospective client, partner, or client asks me "How long will it take to raise capital from investors?" I ALWAYS respond, "It depends." I don't have a magic potion nor a magic book. And even though I have been helping companies raise capital from investors for almost two decades, I will tell you investors can be as unpredictable as Georgia weather. They can be enthusiastic and all on board one minute and disgusted and talking about you the next.

The combination of the factors I named coupled with the interactions they have with the company can bring an investor to a "yes" or a "no." As I always say, capital raising is both an art AND a science. A lot of founders make the mistake of only studying the science portion and that will only get you so far. Still study the science, but just know there are other factors that may not make sense that are involved. We are, of course, talking about humans and human behavior. It's a complicated area of psychology. And I imagine there is so much human psychology that's involved that I am totally unqualified as to speculate as to the exact answer of why investors say no to some investments and yes to others.

Some reasons why...

They want their money back.
But while I don't know the exact, consistent answer to the specific question of how to get an investor "closer to a yes," the root answer to this question is pretty simple: NO ONE wants to lose money. The potential investor may appreciate and even love the energy and founders of Company 1B, but, at the end of the day, investing isn't a hobby. The point of investing is to grow an investor's money. That's it. It's common sense and not earth-

shattering, but there it is. No matter how altruistic you think investors are or should be—no one wants to lose money. It's called "investment" for the very reason that investors want not only their initial investment back but more. And you and I have to admit that seems reasonable—more than reasonable. Investors are taking a risk with something and someone you cannot control both internally with teams and externally with markets and the regulatory environment. It would only follow that, in exchange for that uncertainty and risk, the investor gets back their principal and extra. You would want the same for your investment, so this only makes sense.

As I write this, maybe I did, indeed, answer my own question for the most part, but I believe there are other factors that make hard to get a "yes" from an investor. Maybe reason no. 1 is as simple as I stated: Investors want their money back, and so they hold on to their money until they are completely comfortable parting ways with it. This is connected with trust, which we will discuss later in this book. If I am investing my money with no guarantee of return, it's going to take something more than a cold email and a few faceless calls and a ZOOM to get me to hand over my hard-earned cash. It takes time to develop trust. As I tell clients of Kairos, "Consistent conversations lead to capital." However, even though I don't have the magic formula that will always and quickly get all investors to a "yes," I tell you what I can do: I can tell you what can get them closer to a "yes." I can also tell you why it's so important to get an investor closer to a "yes" as soon as possible.

Market Oversaturation

An additional reason it's hard to get some investors to a "yes" is the fact that the market is saturated with "good ideas." I put "good ideas" in quotes because if you ever talk to a passionate founder, every last founder has a GREAT idea. Company 1B is the next big thing to hit the corporate governance scene—haven't you heard? Founders like Company 1B have an idea you have never seen before and if they could only get an investment.... Every founder you meet will tell you they have the next star-studded, billion-dollar company or unicorn. And every founder SHOULD think that; otherwise, I personally would never invest with them. As a founder, you should think you are headed toward building a great company; otherwise, you will find the road to entrepreneurship frustrating and unfulfilling. But let's look at all these great companies from the standpoint of an investor.

If you are an investor, particularly a community investor where everyone knows you're an investor or even if you are an accredited investor, your name is on some list that's circulating Al Gore's internet. I assure you it is because I get cold solicitations all the time in my email and on LinkedIn. As an investor, you on the mind of the millions of founders around the world, and they are coming for you! As a result, investors have LOTS of investment options—a market oversaturation. And whenever you are overloaded with options, there is paralysis that can set in because you have so many choices. Company 1B is not looking any different than Company 4C in the initial flood of solicitations. It's choice overload!

I remember visiting the Cheesecake Factory for the first time in undergrad at Oglethorpe University in Atlanta, Georgia. I was 18 years old, and I remember the excitement of being out with my friends and not having to let my parents know my every move. I had a job so I was making use of my new debit card, feeling like an adult. (Amazing how fast adulting wears off as a thrill.) I sit down with friends, and the waiter brings us this heavy menu. I was hungry (I usually am), and I couldn't wait to taste this Cheesecake Factory magic everyone was talking about. I get the menu. I open the menu. The menu was somewhere between 10 to 15 pages long! My introvert anxiety set in—I got up and told my friends I would get something else nearby. There were WAY—and I mean WAY—too many options. I was hungry and needed the menu narrowed down to the best options. It would have taken me at least 30 minutes to go through that menu. I didn't have time for that, so I didn't make a choice. Now this example may be an extreme, but you get my drift. Too many choices can lead to not making a choice at all—or at least delaying that choice for a while. The same thing happens to investors daily. The more popular the investor, the more choice overload happens, and the harder it is to get that investor to a "yes."

Other Concerns

I know there are many other reasons you can think of why it's so hard to get a "yes" from investors. Some are biases against a gender, sexual orientation, race, or any number of things. There are literally investors who just think female founders are too emotional to make sound decisions. (Although all wars were started by who? I rest my case.) And to be clear—those biases EXIST. They are there. They are more common than you think and they can even be subconscious, which is worst that intentional in my opinion. But, for purposes of this book, let's remove those barriers and biases.

What I explained above is my perspective of why it's so hard to get investors to say "yes" without the barriers and biases I know exist. Why am I removing those barriers? Because otherwise this book would be useless and probably 100 pages longer. I have no idea how to break through to racist, homophobic, and sexist investors. None. So nothing I say on that subject would be useful except to say "bias exists." And if I tried to explain it, you would be reading this book from now until this same time next year. Bias and discrimination are not my areas of expertise nor my calling—and I don't want them to be. I just am a warrior against them. So my sections above talks about investors in general, removing those biases for the sake of this book.

Why Is It Important

Let's cut to the chase. Getting an investor to say "yes" is important for this main reason: Time is money. You've heard it before, but it's true for a company that's trying to build. If you are talking about your cash runway, i.e., how much cash you have flowing through your company before you run out or about the time value of money, i.e., $1 today is not going to be worth the same amount five years from now—time really is money! So, every "no" you receive delays the "yes" you need in order to bring in much needed funds into your company to get it working for you, your company, and your investors. Getting those dollars in to get to work for your company and the investor is vital to starting the process of growing. With cash, you have options. Options that your competitors may not have and options that will allow you to make the best decision about your company without worrying about how to pay for it. Without cash, you have less options. Less opportunities to be competitive in an already competitive world and less options to expand your company. You want cash. You need cash. Let's get cash.

A secondary reason that it's important to get a "yes" from an investor is because, if you are doing it right, Founders, you are seeking an investor that is not only providing hard capital to you. While cash is king (or queen) and it's the fuel of the company, a savvy investor and founder will know that bringing cash to the relationship is the bare minimum. This is about more than money; this is relationship. Investors can bring so much more to a growing company such as more strategic relationships, including those with future investors, knowledge of a particular industry, and other resources needed to take a company to the next level of serving a particular market. Founders should have a working relationship with their investors that involves having the hard conversations and asking the questions that you want to know. Believe me, investors love it when founders ask for their advice— particularly because their money is on the line! So, ask those questions and get the insight you need to scale your business. The sooner you get an investor to say "yes," the sooner they join you on that train to success as an informal advisor. And THAT— money cannot even buy.

Chapter 4. How To Get Closer to a "Yes"

The moment you have been waiting on is here! That's right—I am actually going to discuss HOW to get you closer to a "yes" from an investor. I thought it was helpful to give you the first three chapters so that you have an appreciation and perspective for the investing ecosystem.

Let me just start off by saying, depending on who you ask, "How do I get an investor to say 'yes' to investing in my company?" you will get all different answers. All I can tell you is what has worked for my clients in the past using the same business coaching method that I use for my law firm. As you know by now, in addition to being a corporate law firm and investment advisory firm in Georgia, my firm offers business coaching services. I added this on as a service offering once I began to realize that my clients and potential clients, all of whom are business owners, were looking for guidance before it was time to hire me as a lawyer. They had the vision of raising capital from investors but needed more guidance about just how to get there, i.e., how to become the most investor-ready they could be so that hiring me wasn't in vain. So, I decided to put my years of legal experience exclusively working with founders, my MBA, my Series 65 license, and my years as an arbitrator to even better use by developing a business coaching program.

Now, I was raised in the black church since the age of 9. I would hear people remark of the preaching *"Take out what's for you and leave the rest."* And rightly so because not every word spoken in a sermon speaks to you and your situation. Use the same guidance here. Every founder, company, situation, industry, investor, and objective are different. My job is to give you the whole buffet and let you decide what you want to put on your plate. I will be taking you through a five-step process to becoming "Investor Ready." If some parts don't apply to you or you already are ready, skip it. But I am going to lay out the entire process for you to fill in the blank. The more you complete and consider my follow-up call to action, the better your results with investors.

My five-step process has a goal of taking you from where you are a founder to where you need to be to be able to raise your first investor dollar on Day 1. That's IF you follow my plan and then act on my plan, including seeking any follow-up assistance you may need. I am just an attorney and business coach, not a magician. I cannot magically manifest investors who are fighting to invest in your business. You have to do the actual work. I can only do the work that I can do—the rest is up to you and your team. So the questions to answer are this: How hungry are you? How good are you at following expert advice? Will you make the hard decisions fast enough to get your first investor dollar? These and many other questions separate those who are on their way to hitting their capital raising target or oversubscribe and those that are still wondering "why not me?" Let's get started. Let's get Company 1B that much needed capital.

My Investor Ready business coaching program is divided into five sessions: (1) foundation; (2) framework; (3) financials; (4) forward thinking; and (5) future. Since that's the way it's divided, it only makes sense to go through this book in that order. My mind works in a linear fashion, and, apparently, I have a thing for alliteration. To set the stage for the next sections of the book, think about this coaching program as building a house—the house of Company 1B. As you already know, houses are not built overnight. They take planning and a process to make sure they are stable and manifest the vision of the developer. If all parts don't work together, you won't have a very attractive or stable house. That's what coaching, any coaching, is meant to do: Transform you from your status now to the status you want to be. That's what the five sessions are meant to do.

My suggestion for getting the most out of this chapter is to download the guide and follow along. I would reach each session first to give an objective of each session so you know what's the purpose in advance of filling out the guide. Then schedule some intentional time to fill out the guide with you and your team. It would be helpful if everyone involved in completing the guide read this book to give perspective. Kairos, my law firm/investment advisory firm, is always available to assist to answer questions and for more personalized attention, as this book alone won't provide you with any coaching services that you may need.

Session 1: Foundation
No surprise here. Before you start on any great journey, particularly one that's as hard as raising capital, you have to get back to the basics. Before you start to build a house, you have the lay a foundation. You have to understand who and what Company 1B wants to project to the outside world. My dad has been in the construction business for over 40 years, and I can tell you, I have seen a LOT of foundations. Some strong and thoughtfully planned and some that seemed like they were an afterthought of the developer.

A company and its founders have to make sure they have laid the groundwork on which everything else with the company will be built, just like a house. Company 1B has to take the time to firmly establish its value system and direction as a company. This will be the roadmap on which every other decision stands. During this process, great companies build their foundation on solid ground and not on sinking sands. So that, when the storms of entrepreneurship and life happen (and I assure you they will), the company is able to stand firm and focus on the mission by knowing who it is and what it is doing. Company 1B, you and others who take this first step will not be moved nor come tumbling down because you've built a strong foundation.

As you can see from the guide (appendix to this book), the deeper purpose of establishing a strong foundation is for the company to REALLY get to know WHO it is before it starts broadcasting to the outside world. Any marketing guru will tell you that we all have a brand, whether we want one or not. That being the case, we have to decide what do we want others to say about us when we aren't in the room. Founders have to get LASER-focused on what they are trying to do, who they are trying to do it for, how they are going to do it and with whom. These are the foundational questions to ask and answer in as much detail as possible.

I tell clients to close their eyes and visualize the ideal client and ideal investor. This visual should look like an actual person with features, clothes, mannerisms, and habits, almost like those cartoon images you can make of yourself on social media. Then, write those characteristics down. It may seem like a silly activity, but you cannot be everything to everyone and every investor. So, take the time to get silent with your team about your company's foundation, what you are about, and whom you are targeting as a client and an investor. This takes time, energy, hard questions, and even harder choices as well as collaborative input from outside counsel. And once founders have answered these questions amongst themselves, they must convey this vision to the entire team. I mean, what's the use in having a massive vision for an entire organization that you keep to yourself or just a few people?

Session 2: Framework
Now that you have established a strong and mighty foundation, now it's time to expand from there. Remember, we are building a house. In Session 1, you laid the slab (or any other foundation you choose for this illustration), and now it's time to put up the wooden frames that will give the house its design. This is where

Company 1B can go into details and get creative. How many rooms will it have? Where will the kitchen be located? Is there a pool out back? Is the primary bedroom separate from the other rooms? Is it a one or two level? Will there be carpet or hardwood floors in this house? This is what the framework session is meant to be and do. It's meant to give structure to your foundation so you can see layout and overall plan for the house's structure. As you build this framework, you should begin to start thinking of how much it's going to cost to build this house as well. That's why the details in the framework are so important.

So how do you make sure that the house looks like how you envisioned it with the right number of rooms and the pool out back and an amazing primary bedroom and bath away from the other rooms? Well, we have to focus on the right processes to build out this plan. This means bringing in the right people to frame the walls and lay the tilework, including but not limited to strategic partners and early employees. This means getting the paperwork together to make sure all parties understand the vision and legally protect the Company 1B from misunderstandings that could slow the process down. Then, finally, you have to present your visual and verbal pitch to others helping you build the house, so visually everyone is on the same page.

Now, as you go through building out this framework, always remember your foundation. It's easy to get discouraged and unfocused during this time in the process because there are so many things happening at once and so many choices to make. You have different people working on your house at different times. Everyone plays a different role and has a different idea about how to build this house. But remember the foundational principles you established in Session 1 that you have conveyed to your team as a founder. Remember your why: why you are building your company; the problem you are solving; and the value system you have established in your company. Company

1B set out to build a house. It doesn't need to end up building an apartment, or a high rise, or a shopping mall—Company 1B is building a house.

That should always be the focus when building out the framework for this building. This house will have certain things an apartment building will not, and it won't have some things a high rise will. That's okay! Because Company 1B is building a house. So, Founders, you have to keep your foundational principles in mind during this session, or you may end up with an apartment building. Now, I am not saying there are not times to pivot. As a matter of fact, flexibility is one of the key components of entrepreneurship as life does happen, and you will have to make changes. But you change the process, not the end goal. You are still building a house, but maybe you have to relocate the guest bathroom to another corner of the house. Keep your foundation in mind as you make daily and long-term decisions.

Session 3: Financials
Well, now that we have a strong foundation and framework for the house we are building, it's now time to figure out how we will pay for the house. This is where investors come in. Company 1B has laid the slab, the frames are up, and the finishes have been chosen. All Company 1B needs now is the money to pay for it all. Therefore, there are important decisions to be made. Is Company 1B going to use debt, equity, or a combination of both? Does Company 1B want to conduct a priced or unpriced round? If it's a priced round, what valuation method (and there are many) will be used? What is Company 1B's past financial performance and how does it put those figures together in a way that are realistic and easy to understand for the investors? These and so many other questions are what you are determining in the financials session of getting "investor ready."

Many clients will ask me if they should hire a full-service CPA firm to do their financial documents for their company to prepare them to raise capital from investors. You aren't going to be surprised by this answer—BUT it depends. CPAs are different and usually charge higher than accountants—and for good reason. CPAs have special training in financial documents and analysis, so they cost more. It all depends on your budget, what regulatory exemption you are using (remember some required professional financial statements), and what you already have. It also depends on how much you are trying to raise and from whom. If you are trying to raise $25 million from institutional and sophisticated investors, then the answer is probably a strong "yes" to hiring a CPA firm. If you are trying to raise a pre-seed round from family and friends of $25,000, then probably "no" to hiring a full-service CPA firm. It's very likely for the latter that you can get a regular accountant to put together that information.

This session is also where you determine what financing regulatory exemption you will be using. Specifically, how will you legally raise capital so that no federal, state, or local entity shuts down your fundraising before you get started. Remember, we discussed the various regulatory exemptions to S.E.C. registration in the previous chapters. This seems self-serving (and it is), but please, PLEASE spend the investment on a highly experienced securities attorney. The attorney that did your cousin's divorce or the one you used for your personal injury case is NOT sufficient. This is a highly regulated, ever-changing area of law, and you don't want to be left wondering why you're in legal trouble with an investor or, even worse, a federal or state agency. Take the time to partner with a great securities attorney so you can work though this particular step of building your house together. At Kairos, we are hired many times to act like "Batman."

For example, Company 1B may have a corporate attorney who handles negotiations and paperwork and the day to day of

Company 1B. But when it comes time to raise capital, Company 1B sends up the Bat Signal because it needs a specialty attorney—and we come to the rescue. When we are done with helping Company 1B raise capital, we disappear back into our Bat Cave. It's the same with this. You wouldn't want an electrician tiling your bathroom floor. You want to make sure you get the attorney who can get this specific aspect of your company done for you.

At the end of the day, the purpose of this session is to answer this vital question to the investor: Will I, when and how, be paid back on my investment with a sizeable return? How much can I expect that to be? You answer this by providing financial information. This includes the financial documents with past performance, future projections, and the legal road map for assuring the investor that the numbers are in order, and there is a path forward for scale and success. Remember that investors are not solely philanthropists out investing money in companies they don't think will be successful. Every single investor I have ever met—ALL, in fact—want to be paid back on their investment and with a return. Otherwise, what's the point of being an investor?

Session 4: Forward Thinking
I bet you are saying at this point: "Seems like I have everything I need for this house to be built." No, you don't. What happens if there are delays in building the house? What if it rains or snows and the contractors cannot do their job? What if the city withholds permitting? What if you or the other builders get sick and have to take time off? What if a supply has a back order longer than you expected? (I clearly have been watching way too much HGTV, but I digress.) You see, life happens, and it happens FAST when you are a founder. Believe me, as a serial founder I know. The unexpected always seems to come at the worse times, too—

when I have built momentum and I can see the light at the end of the tunnel. Sound familiar?

This session, Company 1B is playing the role of a clairvoyant in that it is trying to predict the future and plan a response. What may happen? What will happen? How does the company and team respond? How does the company continue to build as a company? What is the process to make sure that the company continues to focus on its foundational principles and move forward toward the capital raising goal? You need to ask the same questions and even more. These are all important questions to ask NOW, so that when life and entrepreneurship happen, you are prepared.

I cannot underscore enough how important it is to prepare. I know as founder you are daily grinding and thinking about the next meeting or the next day or even the next hour. It can be hard to sit still long enough to think about the "what ifs" and then prepare for those. I get it. You are just trying to survive another day and the payroll still needs to be paid at the end of the month. But, as the saying goes, "proper preparation prevents problems." And it's very true! You can expect the best, but always—ALWAYS—plan for the worse. I am sure there is some principle to support this recommendation. Keep this in mind as you complete this session. It will serve you well in the future. I assure you!

Get with your team and plan for every scenario that you can think of with respect your capital-raising journey. You know the saying, "the house always takes longer and is more expensive to complete than what was originally planned." The same is true with your capital raising journey—that's why I call it a "journey." It's filled with distracting scenic landscapes and mud pits to jump over. Like all the sessions, competing this session will take time and guidance. Don't rush it. Start writing down your thoughts, and as you think about the "what ifs," add them on. Get as much free-flowing input as possible. Beside each possible or expected scenario, write down your process for dealing with that scenario and who is responsible for each task and timeline. Getting as detailed as possible about your plan of attack not only will give you peace of mind as a founder, but it will give your team peace of mind that you are ready for anything and to prevent problems in the future. And, if an investor asks "what if?" you will already be prepared to answer. And how much confidence would that put into the mind of an investor if you already had a solution and plan for a "what if?" That's how you get closer to a "yes."

Session 5: Future

We are finally at the end of this five-step process. You are probably wondering, "What's the difference between the forward-thinking and future" session. Well, I am glad you asked. The forward-thinking session is a snapshot and plan for what to do during this particular capital raise. In essence, how will you build THIS house. This future session is planning for future capital raises so how will you build FUTURE houses or do future raises. Very rarely do companies only do one capital raise and never raise capital again from investors, particularly if they are successful. Therefore, it only makes sense that you map out a more strategic and extensive plan for your interaction with current and probably future investors with your company.

What this future session is doing is planning out how you will foster and keep the relationships with the people who helped you build your first house, so that when you build future houses, you have a smoother process and investors ready to help. Whereas the forward-thinking session can be categorized as more immediate, short-term thinking, this future session is planning for the longer-term future.

In order to plan for future investors, you have to focus on the investors you have now under your current raise. The investment community is very small, so how you treat these investors, as well as prospective investors, will have an impact on future raises. That's why this session is dedicated to ensuring you have a written plan for how you deal with current investors. The decisions and interactions you make today can have either a positive or negative effect on future raises. Why leave it to chance when you can plan to make sure your chances for positive interactions are at their highest with your current investors?

As a founder, you know that relationships matter, and they don't matter any less when you are raising capital from investors. As a matter of fact, I would argue they matter more for the reasons I stated above. As I tell clients all the time, taking money from investors is the START of the relationship not the END. Now that you have their money, you are in a marriage with them. So don't take money from anyone you would not want to be stuck in an elevator alone with for several hours. Yeah—it's like that. So part of your future planning should be the first step, i.e., making sure there is an investor–founder fit in the first place. There are discussions all day about product-market fit, but rarely do coaches spend time on the investor–founder fit like we do in our coaching sessions. Because it's important. Not all money is good money. Choose wisely.

But assuming you want to enter into a business marriage with this investor, and they have invested, how do you treat them like they need to be treated? Maybe not how they want to be treated, as that can be onerous, depending on the investor, but how they need to be treated: Respect includes transparency, honesty, and loyalty to their money.

Finally, once the founders have come up with an investor relations plan, as always, it's important to share with the team.

Because if the investor has a bad experience with a team member, I PROMISE it will reflect on the entire company. Make sure that every interaction a potential or current investors has with someone from your team aligns with the investor relations plan that you have set out. Ideally, this plan would be written and easily accessible to all team members and the highlights repeated frequently. Let's prevent future problems, particularly with investors, with proper planning.

Conclusion

This is the grand finale. You have completed your plan. This is your plan. If you have followed along with the guide and taken my suggestion about how to complete this chapter, you should have a written document that is a powerful statement and template to build on in the coming weeks. Each session, as listed above, is meant to build steadily and strategically on one another so that, by the time you are done, you have a guide that you can revise and share and take you through the capital-raising process. Again, this takes patience and deep thought and collaboration. You can do it! Start NOW! There is no better time like the present to build that beautiful house.

Chapter 5. So, What Now?

I can read your thoughts. Your thoughts are saying, "Okay, Dar'shun. What now? I have this written guide that I have toiled over for weeks or months. I have shared it with my team. I have updated it and refined it so it's a well-oiled machine. So what do I do now? What do I do with this lovely guide that's so filled with words? How do I put it into action? I don't want to be like the founder you mentioned before who has a piece of paper with a plan but doesn't execute that plan. How do I get this capital raising party started?" This chapter answers that and many other questions, so listen closely and take notes.

First, let me point out that these are all great questions. There's no point in having a guide if it doesn't do any guiding, right? In this chapter, I will discuss with you some best practices for finding investors. Many prospective clients think that Kairos offers this as an independent service, but we don't. We are not broker-dealers, so we don't do investor introductions outside of the casual ones we give to our premium clients. Sorry. So that means that you are still tasked with finding investors. It's best this way anyway. Company 1B's founders are in the best position to know what investor fits their company anyway. Remember what I said about founder–investor fit? It's a thing (or should be a thing).

If you have visualized your ideal investor, as I suggested in the last chapter, you know EXACTLY what your ideal investor looks like. Take the avatar that you created in your mind and wrote down visually on paper. All these characteristics will come to life and become helpful in this chapter.

My Top 5 Best Practices

As I go through these best practices, please remember that these are suggestions I give my clients. But remember the advice I gave about the preacher giving a sermon. Take that same advice and apply it here.

Best Practice No. 1

Keep in mind and write down this phrase: *"Consistent conversations lead to capital."* Put it on an index card, write it on the entrance to your company building, have the founders go out and tattoo it on their arms—whatever works! Company 1B's founder could put this phrase in their email signature or start team meetings with this reminder. Getting a check in your hand always takes longer and sometimes is smaller than you, as a founder, would like it to be. Always. So, it's important FIRST to get your mindset right as a founder and get your team's mind in a place of persistence. It is my hallmark principle for clients of my firm. When you are raising capital, it is very easy to get discouraged. (Entrepreneurship in general is one big roller coaster without the added pressure of securing capital—amen?)

Things rarely go the way that you want them to go, including pitches to investors. Meetings rarely are as short as you expect them to be. And the checks never come in as fast and large as you'd like. But, through all this, remember what we talked about: Why it's hard to raise capital from investors in the first place. I almost guarantee it will take more conversations than you think to get an investor to meet with you or return your calls or to say yes and even to write that check. But be consistent in your conversations. That means do the hard parts and make the connections every day, even when you don't want to. That also means having those meaningful conversations—and not all of them have to be about pitching your business. Investors are people, too, with interests and needs. Take advantage of connecting on a personal level. Not too personal but just enough that the investor sees you are founder acting like a friend. Consistent conversations always lead to capital.

Best Practice No. 2
Now that we have the cerebral part of finding investors out of the way, let's concentrate on the practical. Use the Tupperware bowl method to write out your list of perspective investors. Once you have done this, you can make a plan to connect so you start to implement Best Practice No. 1. When I first ran for political office and had to raise money, which I feared more than death, someone suggested this activity. The goal is to start from your innermost circle and build larger audiences, like larger Tupperware bowls, until your list gets bigger and broader. You start with the people closest to you like your family and friends. They are the smallest bowl of a Tupperware set. Then, you contact colleagues who you work with at a job or interact daily. That's the 2nd biggest Tupperware bowl. Next, list out associates, people that you know from community organizations and professional affiliations. That's your 3rd biggest Tupperware bowl. Next may be friends of family or friends of friends and acquaintances, making it your 4th biggest Tupperware bowl. Finally, your 5th Tupperware bowl is the general public, people you absolutely don't know. Hopefully, you get the point of this exercise.

Then, once you have this Tupperware bowl of investors built out, confirm two questions from everyone in those layers: (1) Who has disposable income to invest (the ABILITY to invest); and (2) Who would be interested in what you are offering (the WILLINGNESS to invest). Answering these two questions comes from your knowledge of people in the innermost Tupperware circle. The answers also come from research for those who are further outside of the core Tupperware bowl. Answering these two questions are important because it makes no sense to spend time on investors who either can't invest or don't want what you are selling. If Company 1B is a fintech company and keeps approaching an angel investor who invests in only real estate, Company 1B is wasting its time trying to convince this angel to invest in its company. As a company, you must get laser-focused on the investor you visualized in the earlier chapter.

Best Practice No. 3
Tell your story. Every founder has a story that is uniquely their own or they can tell in a unique way. Lean into that! When you tell your story, investors get insight not only into how you are as a person but why you are who you are. That's powerful! Because it tells the story of motivation and character in a way that a pitch deck or website never could. For example, my parents are the reason that I am a corporate attorney, as I detailed in the first chapter. They are my inspiration and why I particularly love to help female founders and founders of color. The fact that I was able to take the lessons I learned watching them build their business into something informative for other founders is a story I love to share. Not only is it worth sharing, but it speaks to others in a heartfelt way because, good or bad, we are all affected by our childhood upbringing, which will resonate with others.

I see many founders try to copy what some other successful founder has done. And I get it! Why recreate the wheel of what seems to have already worked? But here's the thing to remember: Every founder journey is different. It's the little things in your business plan or your team or your product or service that can change the course of you raising capital from investors. So embrace what makes you unique and use it for your advantage. Don't shy away from what makes you stand out---investors like that actually! You can take some parts of what has worked in the past for others but don't make it your entire story. You are different and that's why you are doing what you are doing. Embrace it!

Best Practice No. 4
Show up every day and do the hard parts. One aspect of this is Best Practice No. 1, which is to have consistent conversations with potential investors. But to have these conversations, you have to show up. Show up where potential investors, who are specifically able and willing to invest in your company, hang out. That means getting uncomfortable and entering rooms you otherwise would not. That means a sacrifice of time and energy as you enter the space of where your potential investors are in the world. Investors are at trade shows and conferences and smaller networking groups and organizations. Find those leads that match your industry, and you will find potential investors. Do it all and do it consistently.

You are building a company. Founders, you will never grow inside of your comfort zones. You aren't satisfied with a side hustle product or service but instead want to build something special that offers the world a solution to a problem. That won't be easy. You have to convince the right market that you have the right solution to the right problem at the right time. That takes long nights, research, asking the hard questions, making the hard decisions and committing to doing whatever it takes daily to move toward your goals. This means foregoing the night out with friends to practice your pitch with your team for an important investor meeting the next morning. Laying out the specific objectives and benchmarks in the coaching guide is so important because it keeps you focused on what you need to be doing daily, weekly, monthly, annually and everything in between. If you don't know where you are going and work every day to get there, you will end up in a place you don't want to be or don't recognize. Don't let that be you.

Best Practice No. 5

Surround yourself with a superstar team. The No. 1 reason that investors invest in a company, no matter what they tell you, is the team. That can be a solo founder or a few founders. Investors do not care if you have the next Calendly or Goodr Nation. Remember what I said earlier? That great ideas abound everywhere, particularly for investors. But you know what is scarce? Hard work and grit. Investors are looking for a team that is knowledgeable and committed to turning a start-up company into a successful company that can return the investor's money. Ideas without proper execution are often useless dreams.

Now you are probably thinking, "I don't have money for great teams. That's why I need to raise capital." Get creative. Find a way. If you have an experienced securities attorney on your team, they have seen this scenario plenty of times. They should be able to advise on alternative ways to get you to the team you need with the bare minimum of cash flowing out of your company. You need that cash flow as you build. I get it! But great companies don't build into successful companies with cash; they build with great teams who use the cash to build. A VERY important added bonus of having an experienced securities attorney on your team is also because they can let you know about dilution, i.e., what that means for you as a founder. They should be able to take you through the math so that you understand how much company you will have left after raising a round. So commit to getting a team that can bring your vision to fruition through hard work, hard conversations, and hard choices. If you do this, you are well on your way to getting to a "yes."

What Do Investors REALLY want?

Depends. (You knew that answer was coming.) But seriously—it does. Investors are humans driven by human psychology and behavior just like me and you. What makes one investor say "yes" and the next say "no" and the next not even return your calls is a mystery to me. But I have tried to put together at least some general points about what investors REALLY want to see from companies that will move them closer to a "yes."

Let me start off my generally saying what they DO NOT want—confusion! You confuse, you lose. Remember my mention about why it's so hard to get investors to a "yes"? They are bombarded with "offers" all the time. So, if you are confusing them on top of sending them your offer, they are out. Another deal is waiting in their inbox. And this lesson is something we all consider in our interactions. How many of you have clicked off a website for a purchase because you just couldn't figure out how to make a purchase? Or left a lecture or seminar because the speaker's thought process and words were all over the place, and you couldn't follow? Or delayed a task from a colleague or superior because you just didn't know what they wanted you to do? You confuse, you lose. Make it simple and easy. That's what the coaching guide is meant to do—provide clarity.

➢ **To see a strong team.** This seems obvious, but you'd be surprised how many founders don't REALLY get this. As I tried to emphasize repeatedly, great ideas are all around us. The difference between Tope Awotona creating Calendly and me continuing to use a Google form to schedule appointments is his team. Teams create great companies—not money, not technology, not a plan. Actual, living human beings that can do the work and make things happen. So, focus No. 1 on your team of those who are helping you build your business. And I don't only mean early employees. During our business coaching sessions, we spend time with founders to decide if they need a co-founder and the type of co-founder needed to scale the business. Statistically, it's easier to raise with a co-founder, but, just like an investor-founder fit, you still need a co-founder fit. That plus time and the process of specifically identifying what the current founder brings to the table and what is lacking as well as visualizing the type of co-founder you want. If you have already solidified a co-founding team, this is even more important! Now is the time to align your commitment, interests, goals and everything in between so that you present a united front to the world and to potential investors.

- **To See Your Vision.** As I stated previously, once you confuse, you lose. That goes for clients and investors alike. The investor wants you to lay out, in the simplistic terms, HOW you are going to get your company from where you are to where they need you to be to realize a return on their investment. You can do this a variety of ways, e.g., through pitches and decks and portals with additional information. But putting things in writing and pitching may not be enough. They may require that you have a working prototype or that you have done a focused group survey or that you have paid users to build traction. That's why it's so important to do research on your investor. All investors do not communicate or make investment decisions the same. If you are having those consistent conversations I talked about, you should have some sense of their communication style and what will take them closer to saying "yes" to your investment based on their questions, past investments or for others who know their investment style.

- **To See Their ROI.** Even if you have a strong team and vision, investors still want to know how they will get their money back. Their investment isn't a charitable donation they are looking to do in your business. They are looking for returns of their principal AND additional capital. Much of this will turn to your financial documents and projections, which we assist you with during our coaching session. But a good portion of this will also turn on the written plan in your offering document. You need to explain how your product or service fits the specific need of the market you are in and, if it fits, how will you bring it to market so everyone knows you exist.

  What is your plan to make revenue? Subscriptions? User experience? Programs? Sponsorships? A combination? Then, do all of these factors to justify the financial projections you have one, three, or five years from now. I caution founders that just because you put on an excel projection that you will be $20MM in Year 1 doesn't make it true, and any investor would look for the data and plan to back that up.

- **To See You As Honest.** I mentioned earlier that if you, as a founder, do not want to be stuck in an elevator with an investor, you should probably turn down their money. Well, I offer that advice to investors and general partners at funds as well. At the end of the day, we are all humans who expect decent interactions with each other as humans. The same is true, if not more, in the private capital market space. We are talking about private capital markets which, by their very name, as less regulated and less transparent than dealing with companies and investors in public capital markets. So human decency and character mean even MORE in the private capital markets because the stakes are higher than they are in a public market.

For some investors, it may be enough to have a great idea with a great plan and a great team. That's all they need. But, in my experience, if you are a dishonest and shady founder, or any of your co-founders are such, or even perceived as being less than a decent human being, it's very hard to get an investor to hand you over their hard-earned money. They don't trust you. They may trust the company, but the company needs you to execute and run the company. So, if they can't trust you, they can't trust what the company could be. You can't really blame them. We do business with people we like right? So why wouldn't we expect the same for people we don't like?

➤ **To See You Have It Together (Financially and Legally).** This is self-serving, but I am going to say it anyway. Any decision you make as a founder will have one of two consequences and, sometimes, particularly when you are raising capital, both: (1) a financial consequence; and/or (2) a legal consequence. Experienced and savvy investors know this. So they want to make sure you have people on your team who can handle these two aspects since every decision you make will affect one of these two areas or both. Additionally, it just gives credence to the fact that you and your team are serious about building an actual company and not a side hustle.

I had a prospective client who was going through an accelerator and wanted to use the accelerator staff for legal documents for his raise. I said, "okay." But when you are having consistent conversations with potential investors, which do you think sounds more powerful: "Yeah, I'll have the accelerator staff prepare those documents" or "I will have my securities attorney prepare those documents." Listen, all I can do is advise. You are your own brand, and you have to decide is your brand going to be. It can be one in which investors go back and talk to each other and say "Founder 1B has their stuff together." Or something else? The choice is yours.

➢ **To See the Exit.** You are building a company, and I am sure the last thing on your mind is 7–10 years from now. But this is an important question for investors because an exit is the way they are going to get their money back and more. There are two types of exits in which an investor will be repaid: (1) An IPO (initial public offering); or (2) an acquisition, where your company is a target of another larger company that purchases your entire company to be wholly consumed by the purchasing company. To keep the math simple, let's say an early investor purchased 15% of Company 1B with a $10,000 investment. After Company 1B completes several capital raising rounds, the investor's ownership is now diluted to 11.37% of Company 1B. I know this sounds random, but this is how dilution works as you raise capital rounds—your experienced securities attorney can walk you through the math.

Carrying on, Company 1B gets acquired by a company for $1M. Since this investor at the time owns 11.37% of the company, they would receive a cash payment of $113,700. This assumes they have preferred stock, and it's not subordinate to anything like debt or a preferred SAFE stock and a few other things. But, to keep it simple, that's how this investor would get paid back on their investment from an acquisition. I don't work with companies doing IPOs, but I'd imagine it's a similar math equation for when a company does an IPO. So you see, the investor is looking for the light at the end of the tunnel to see when and how they will get paid back on their investment. It may have the same outcome for an IPO or an acquisition, but the timeline, due diligence, amount, and decisions by the founder to get to a particular exit will be different. Those factors are important to investors when considering in what companies to invest.

So there you have it. My best practices as well as some high-level discussions about what investors want. This should start you off on your capital-raising journey and allow you to continue to build out the plan that works for you and your company. Nothing that I have spoken about here will be a panacea for flooding investors fighting to write you a check. But each piece is a piece in the puzzle of why investors say yes and designed to get YOU closer to a "yes."

Chapter 6. My Sincerest Wishes for You and Beyond

I decided to write this last chapter to deeply connect with each and every founder who is reading this book. The goal is to take the words off the page and transcend them into a practical conversation, just between me and you. I want you to feel like we are curled up on a couch in your office or living room, having a heart-to-heart conversation about life, liberty, and the pursuit of happiness through entrepreneurship. This is the time that I show you what I consider one of my most IMPORTANT jobs at Kairos—as chief motivation officer or CMO.

As you can imagine, since I only work with founders, particularly those who have made the brave decision to raise capital from investors, there are a lot of times clients want to give up. For all the reasons I lay out in this book and far more than you can imagine, capital raising is a journey and a hard one. That's just the truth. And I believe in being as transparent and as truthful as I can be. And if you are black founder, this capital raising journey is often harder than what your white male counterparts may go through. And if you are a black woman or LatinX woman founder, three to four times harder than that, like a rock. Just when you thought it wasn't possible to get harder than a rock—enter data that show the disparities in different racial groups and genders raising capital in the private markets.[4]

---

[4] S.E.C. Small Business Capital Formation Advisory Committee Report. https://www.sec.gov/about/divisions-offices/office-advocate-small-business-capital-formation/small-business-capital (last assessed 7/25/24). See "FY 2023 Annual Report," pages 43–62.

Because of the reasons above, I have a special place in my heart for female founders and founders of color, particularly black women. No surprise there, but I have a unique connection to all the wonderful black women making a difference in our community like **Veronica Woodruff** of Travelsist and **Kathryn Finney**, Angel Investor and General Partner, and **Jewel Burks Solomon** of Collab Capital and **Jasmine Crowe** of Goodie Nation and **Shila Burney** of Zane Access or **Ryan Wilson** of the Gathering Spot, all of whom proudly hail from **Atlanta, Georgia**. I want to give them their flowers because they are going through battles no one knows and handling it with grace and determination as they move forward to build a successful company for future generations.

Here is my wish for all of you, no matter your background, gender, race or what stage of growth you are in your company: Persist. Persist despite. Persist. Despite whatever [fill in the blank] or whomever. Persist despite whatever or whomever may come or go. In all things and in all ways, persist. It's no secret that the one thing every successful entrepreneur has in common is this: They never gave up. It doesn't mean they don't take the advice of wise counsel or that they did it on their own or that they didn't pivot when necessary. But, when they did have to pivot, they changed the sail or maybe even the direction but never the destination. Remember, Founders, that someone in need is waiting on you to be obedient to your calling. It's something I remind myself of every day as I get up and approach each new day and continue to do the hard parts. Remember the same.

Every day, I want you to picture your future self as you want him or her to be. Take a few minutes to breath in and out and see yourself on a world stage or meeting that person you always wanted to meet or seeing the smile on a customer's face that your product helped make their lives a little better. THAT is why you are doing this! THAT is why you are sacrificing your limited time here on Earth—not with family and friends as you could choose but with your company! While I do believe in making family and friends a priority in life, don't let anyone let you feel guilty for what you are doing. You are BUILDING something special like when my dad lays his worn hands on ceramic tile to build the most beautiful designs in the homes of his customers. Keep building day by day and piece by piece. One day you will have the masterpiece you desire. And years from now you will look back and be thankful for the lessons learned as you built this wonderful masterpiece called your company.

Yes, this is a "you can do it" speech. It's a speech that I love to give and am used to giving. At the end of the day, I am useless as legal counsel if I cannot help provide you with the inspiration you need to keep going as a Founder. Ultimately, you are the "master of your fate and captain of your soul,"[5] but I can help when needed and wanted. I consider it an honor to do so for each one of you Founders. Take care and let's raise that capital!

---

[5] From the poem *Invitcus* by William Ernest Henly (written in 1875 and published in 1888).

Conclusion. Resources & Follow Up

A Personal Note From Dar'shun

I hope that you enjoyed this book and felt every pulse of my passion with every word that you read. If we can ever be of service to you at Kairos, remember we have two coaching programs: (1) An on-demand, self-paced "Investor Ready" course; and (2) Our one-on-one "Investor Ready" coaching program. It would be an honor to work with you to solidify your plan to get you closer to a "yes" from investors.

Other Resources

1. S.E.C. Capital Raising Building Blocks Webpage: https://www.sec.gov/resources-small-businesses/capital-raising-building-blocks/ready-raise-capital
2. Pitchbook Data: www.pitchbook.com
3. Kairos Coaching Programs: www.KairosLegalAdvisors.com/group-coaching

Session No. 1

FOUNDATION

Goal: To assess WHERE I AM as a company NOW so Kairos Capital can guide me to WHERE I NEED TO BE by asking overall questions about my company.

➢ What is my product or service?

_____
_____
_____

➢ What is the problem in the market? (gap in services/product or extent of services/product)

_____
_____
_____

➢ The precise problem my product or service is solving is

_____
_____
_____

➢ Three benefits of my product or service are:
1. _____
2. _____
3. _____

➢ I have proven that my product or service solves a problem and wanted in the marketplace because

_____
_____
_____

_____

- Who are my top-three competitors?
1) _____
2) _____
3) _____
- I am different than my competitors because

_____
_____
_____

- My ideal clients:
- Are mostly ( ) male ( ) female or ( ) both
- between the ages of _____ and _____
- Live in _____
- And are typically _____ (marital status)
- With these other attributes:

_____
_____

- My mission statement (Why do you exist?):

_____
_____
_____

- My vision statement (Your aspirational hopes for the future):

_____
_____
_____

- Therefore, my verbal pitch (30-second elevator pitch) is:

_____
_____
_____
_____

➢ Therefore, my written pitch (longer) is:

_____
_____
_____
_____
_____

➢ What is my TAM (Total Addressable Market), the total amount of potential demand in your market?
_____

➢ What is my SAM (Servicable Addressable Market), the total amount of TAM you can service?
_____

➢ What is my SOM (Servicable Obtainable Market), the total amount of SAM I can service based on my business model?
_____

I will be able to let my ideal customers know about my product or service through a strategic marketing and advertising campaign by…[What is my "Go To Market" Plan?]

Session No. 2

FRAMEWORK

Goal: To put in place the necessary PEOPLE, PARTNERS, PROCESSES, PITCHDECK. and PAPERWORK for me to have a successful raise and beyond.

People

Assemble your Superstar team of Founders AND advisors

Who's on your team now?	Function	Who do you want on your team?	Function

Partners

Who are the partners in the delivery chain you need to bring your product/service to market?

Who are you engaged with now?	Function	Who do you want to engage with?	Function

Processes *I suggest putting these in a separate document and sharing.
- ...for how the founders handle conflict?
- ...for how to deal with emergencies within the supply chain or otherwise?
- ...from start to finish delivering your product/service to the end user?
- ...for on boarding employees/independent contractors?
- ...for vetting potential investors?
- ...for receiving investor funds?

Pitch Deck[6]
1. Keep it under 15 slides, 10 slide ideally.
2. Speak for less than 20 minutes.
3. Be clear! Be clear! Be clear! All through the presentation. ("If you confuse, you lose.")
4. Have simple visuals and statements; less words.
5. Focus on 5 Fs: Foundation; Framework; Financials; Forward-Thinking; and Future (or some variation within)
6. Practice for a GREAT opening and GREAT closing.
7. Be optimistic but not TOO optimistic where it's lying or misrepresentation.
8. Include your ASK and your contact information, particularly if you have a website with more information.

*This page can be used to evaluate each investor's OFFER
1. **Is the OFFER in writing?**
    a. If no, ask for investor to put in writing (1) amount offering to investor, (2) percentage of equity required,

---

[6] We can help with the legal disclaimers of the pitch deck and we have partners that can develop the visuals. I suggest waiting until AFTER our coaching session to finalize this.

(3) type of investment, (4) terms,[7] and (5) any contingencies.
   b. If yes, go to Step 2.
2. **Are you willing to consent to ALL the terms of the written offer?**
   a. If no, counteroffer investor after consulting with us. If you cannot get the minimum terms you want, REJECT OFFER.
   b. If yes, go to Step 3.
3. <u>**Is this investor someone you would not mind being stuck in an elevator with for 5 hours or have dinner with once a week?**</u>
   a. If no, REJECT OFFER.
   b. If yes, go to Step 4.
4. **Are there any "due diligence" red flags to consider? (Reputation of company or individual)**
   a. If yes, REJECT OFFER.
   b. If no, go to Step 5.

Send potential investor legal documents and offer to answer any questions if you make it through ALL steps.

Paperwork
File your regulatory paperwork with the applicable agencies[8] (revise after Session 3 if unknown)
✓   Who do I need to file with?

_____
_____
_____

---

[7] Terms include but not limited to: (1) liquidating preference; (2) board seat; (3) preferred voting rights or dividends; (4) anti-dilution provisions; and (5) communication preferences

[8] Can be federal, state or both depending on financing compliance strategy

- ✓ What do I need to file?

Draft your internal legal documents[9] to present to potential investors vendors, founders, employees, or independent contractors
- ✓ The Offering Document
- ✓ Subscription Agreement
- ✓ Investor Agreement
- ✓ Corporate documents like bylaws, partnership, etc.
- ✓ NDAs (Nondisclosure Agreements)
- ✓ Nonsolicitation Agreements
- ✓ Founders' Agreement
- ✓ Employee Contract
- ✓ Independent Contractor Agreement
- ✓ Vendor Agreement
- ✓ Other based on concerns:

---

[9] REMEMBER, legal services are included in your coaching services.

Session No. 3

FINANCES

Goal: To complete my four financial documents needed for investors to make an informed decision about investing with me and to understand and know those numbers.

Breakdown: Expenses, Costs, and Fees

Expenses/Cost/Fee	Conservative Estimate	Liberal Estimate

TOTAL: $_____ $_____

TOTAL RAISE GOAL: I need to raise $_____ (liberal estimate) by _____ (deadline). I am willing to give up _____% of my business based on a $_____ pre money valuation ESTIMATE.
NOTE: This valuation may have to be changed later.

Benchmark $ Goal	Deadline	Objective (to Reach Benchmark)	Tasks to Reach Objective
Ex. $50,000 (out of $250,000)	June 1	Host an accredited investors brunch	1. Book location, date and time 2. Have admin send electronic invites (4–6 weeks out) 3. Go over agenda with team (1 week out) 4. Prepare materials (3 weeks out)

Determine Your Financing Strategy (for compliance reasons). We will raise capital from investors by the following offering:

- ☐ Federal crowdfunding (Reg. CF)
- ☐ Intrastate crowdfunding (IGE or other)
- ☐ Reg. A+
- ☐ Reg. D: 504
- ☐ Reg. D: 506(B)
- ☐ Reg. D: 506©

Obtain a professional valuation of your business (update above if needed)[10]

_____

The Four "Horsemen" Financial Documents: If not complete, refer.

💲 Cash flow statement (   )

💲 Use of funds (   )

💲 P & L statement (   )

💲 SE equity (   )

_____

[10] From a qualified partner

Session No. 4

FORWARD THINKING

Goal: To develop a written plan to scale my business in such a way and time period that makes investors want to invest in my company.

- Schedule time to meet with your team to go over this document once completed[11]
- Make any revisions to this document, **in consultation with us**, that you deem necessary[12]
- Add benchmarks and objectives from this document, as well as actual document, to shared calendar and system; check in consistently
- My team will be able to execute on scaling this business by

_____
_____
_____
_____
_____

- Benchmarks for SCALE

Year	Objective	Benchmark
1		
2		
3		

---

[11] We can lead team in discussion at our hourly rate for a minimum of 3 hours.

[12] You are allowed 1 FREE revision and afterwards at our hourly rate.

4		
5		
6		

Session No. 5

FUTURE

Goal: To implement "Best Practices" for dealing with investors and issues AFTER the raise and as my company grows.

***Example of graphic for pitch deck**

- Monthly Email Update
- As needed or quarterly investor meetings
- Yearly Written Reports/Audits
- Immediate email alerts when significant issues arise with company that affect investment

Our Communication Promise

- What are the attributes of your IDEAL investor (temperament, how they communicate, how they handle stress, their background, etc.)

  _____
  _____
  _____
  _____
  _____

- Will you need to communicate with some investors more than others? If so, which investors?

  _____
  _____
  _____

- How and how often will you communicate with the above-mentioned investors?

  _____
  _____
  _____

- Who will be responsible for said communication with above mentioned investors?

  _____
  _____
  _____

- Is the above-mention person responsible for ALL investor communications?

  _____
  _____
  _____

- What do future investors in your company look like?

  _____

Let's Develop Written "Best Practices for Investor Relations" Plan for Your Team

*REMINDER: Share this document with your team, reiterate its content often, and update your team anytime there is an update.

www.ingramcontent.com/pod-product-compliance
Lightning Source LLC
Chambersburg PA
CBHW072052230526
45479CB00010B/844